WEEKEND
GUIDE

Points of Interest and Walks Along the Paved Roads of Anza~Borrego Desert State Park

Words & Pictures by Paul R. Johnson

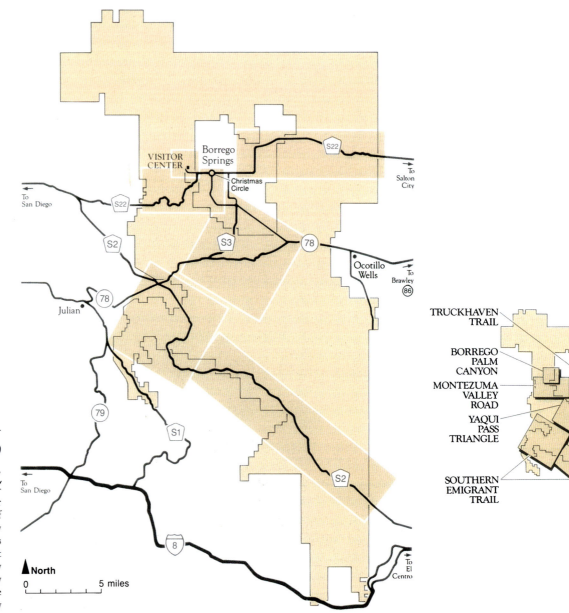

Anza-Borrego Desert State Park

The maps in this publication are for illustrative purposes to convey points of interest along paved roads and a very limited number of dirt roads. The maps are not intended to define the exact boundaries or jurisdiction of any government agency or private property ownership. Boundary lines change frequently, and these maps only approximate current boundaries.

CONTENTS

About This Book	Page 1
Borrego Palm Canyon	Page 3
Montezuma Valley Road	Page 7
Truckhaven Trail	Page 11
Yaqui Pass Triangle	Page 17
Southern Emigrant Trail	Page 23
Index	Page 32

WEEKENDER'S GUIDE

Ocotillos at base of San Ysidro Mountains

ABOUT THIS BOOK

Anza-Borrego Desert State Park is the largest state park in western America. It stretches 60 miles from north to south, 30 miles from east to west, and contains 12 wilderness areas. Within the park's 600,000 acres there are three county roads (S-2, S-3, and S-22), one state highway (78), more than 500 miles of dirt roads, two dozen hiking trails, and a myriad of canyons beckoning the visitor who seeks a quiet place to walk. Finding your way around Anza-Borrego can be confusing for the first-time visitor.

This book is a guide to points of interest, hiking and nature trails, and suggested walks found along the paved roads and selected dirt roads of Anza-Borrego. With a few well-identified exceptions, all of the destinations covered in this guide are accessible by paved road. Four-wheel drive is not required.

In this guide, the park is subdivided into five areas: Borrego Palm Canyon, Montezuma Valley Road, Truckhaven Trail, Yaqui Pass Triangle, and the Southern Emigrant Trail. Each of these areas is described in a separate chapter containing a map, descriptions of trails and points of interest, and photographs. In addition, a map of the entire park, showing the relative position of each area, appears opposite the Table of Contents.

Mile markers like this one appear on County Roads S2, S3, and S22.

Each area map includes the location of highway mile-markers which are posted along the paved roads. Where necessary, written directions are given using landmarks and mile-markers as reference points. In all other cases, you should be able to locate destinations by noting their position on the map in relation to the mile-markers. Distances are given in miles.

Culp Valley, Blair Valley Side Trip, and Mountain Palm Springs are the suggested destinations which require driving on dirt roads. These roads are normally open to any kind of passenger vehicle, but a heavy rainstorm can make them temporarily impassable. Signs warning of dangerous road conditions are sometimes knocked down or removed. A chart of current road conditions is maintained at the Visitor Center. For your safety, check with the Visitor Center or call the park office before venturing down any dirt road in the park, especially after a heavy storm.

WEEKENDER'S GUIDE

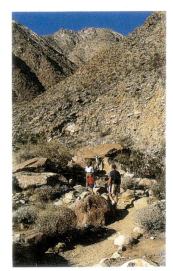

Hikers on the Borrego Palm Canyon Nature Trail

Indian Head Mountain marks the entrance to Borrego Palm Canyon.

BORREGO PALM CANYON

Anza-Borrego's popular Borrego Palm Canyon area encompasses the park's largest campground, visitor center, four walking trails, a natural palm oasis, campfire center, two picnic areas, two pupfish ponds, and administrative headquarters.

VISITOR CENTER

Constructed in 1979, the Visitor Center is partly underground and designed to blend into the desert. Only the east wall, faced with rock from nearby mountains, is exposed. Open seven days a week from October through May (weekends only June through September), the building is the park's information and education center. It contains exhibits on natural and cultural history and offers several different multi-media programs on a variety of desert-related subjects. The sales area offers a wide selection of publications on desert subjects, as well as hiking-related supplies. Volunteers assist uniformed park staff in orienting visitors and answering questions.

California Fan Palm

In the Newt and Mary Ann Williams Garden surrounding the Visitor Center many shrubs and trees native to Anza-Borrego are identified, and a pond offers an opportunity to see the rare desert pupfish.

An easy walk south from the parking lot brings you to a picnic area shaded by native palm trees.

WALKING TRAILS

Starting in the campground near campsite 71, the *Panoramic Overlook Trail* climbs one-half mile to the top of a nearby ridge. Although steep and strenuous, the trail leads to an overlook which provides a sweeping view of the Borrego Valley. Some hikers continue beyond the overlook for a strenuous climb up the side of San Ysidro Mountain.

Borrego Palm Canyon Nature Trail takes you to a beautiful palm oasis with lots of shade and a small stream. This well-traveled trail involves a 1½-mile moderate uphill hike, one way, to the grove. While the quantity of water varies with seasonal rainfall, in winter

WEEKENDER'S GUIDE

— Paved Road
--- Foot Trail
• Point of Interest
⛺ Picnic Area
▲ Campground

These maps only approximate current boundaries.

Coyotes inhabit Borrego Palm Canyon and many other areas of the park.

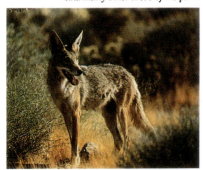

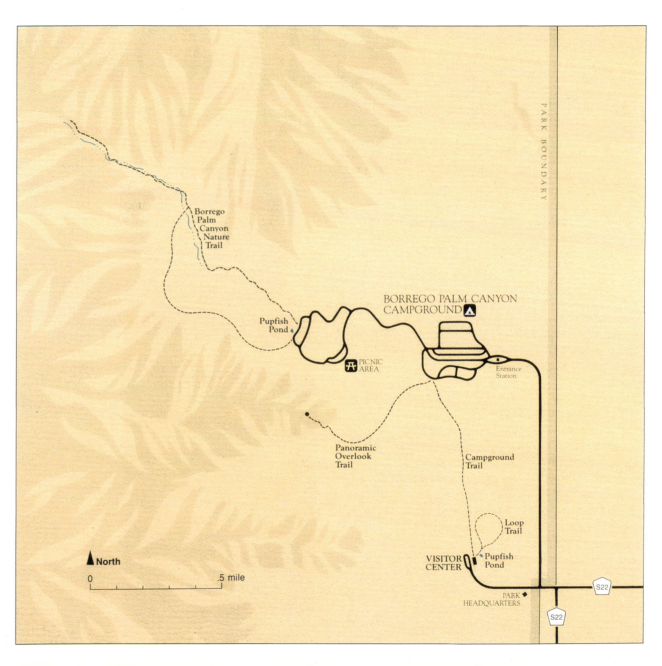

and early spring a creek beside the trail and small waterfall at the upper end of the palm grove are usually flowing. Along the first mile a self-guiding nature trail introduces desert plants, geology, and animals, and offers a glimpse at how Native Americans lived in this desert. A brochure is available at the trailhead. About a quarter mile before it reaches the palm grove, the trail forks. The left branch swings to the south, climbs a low ridge, and then returns through rocky terrain with different plant species.

Two walking paths, the *Visitor Center All-Access Nature Trail* and the *Visitor Center-Campground Trail*, begin at the Visitor Center. The first is a nearly level 0.25 miles loop trail, which begins near the front doors of the Visitor Center. It has a smooth dirt surface and is designed for all-access use. The second connects the campground with the Visitor Center via a textured concrete, slightly inclined trail that is 0.6 miles in length, one-way. Both offer interpretive panels explaining the natural history of the desert.

PUPFISH SANCTUARIES

Beside the parking lot at the Borrego Palm Canyon trailhead is a small pond containing desert pupfish. Recently placed on the federal endangered species list, the Salton Sea pupfish was originally known to live in the Salton Sea and its tributary streams, in San Sebastian Marsh, and in the Fish Creek area of Anza-Borrego Desert State Park. A flood in the early 1900s eliminated the population in Fish Creek, and exotic fish introduced into the Salton Sea have greatly reduced that population. To assist the survival of this species, Anza-Borrego park officials have established several sanctuary ponds. In addition to the one at the Borrego Palm Canyon Trailhead, there is a second pond a few yards from the Visitor Center entrance.

Unique among fish, the pupfish can tolerate water which fluctuates from near freezing to 108 degrees Fahrenheit, and which ranges from fresh to as salty as the ocean. The pupfish is a remnant of the Ice Age, and the few species which survive today are found only in widely scattered, isolated water holes in deserts of the American West.

CAMPFIRE CENTER AND INTERPRETIVE ACTIVITIES

Evening programs are offered at the campfire center from early November through May. Nature walks are also conducted during these months, usually on weekends and during holiday periods. A schedule of interpretive activities is available at the Visitor Center and the park office, and is published in the park newspaper.

PICNIC AREA AND PARK HEADQUARTERS

A large picnic area with tables, shade ramadas, and restrooms is located about a half mile inside the campground. A day-use fee is charged at the entrance station.

Anza-Borrego is part of the Colorado Desert District, which has its headquarters along the Visitor Center entrance road. It is open Monday through Friday from 8:00 A.M. to 5:00 P.M.

BORREGO PALM CANYON

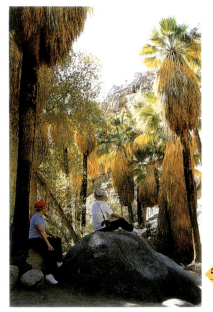

Palm grove, Borrego Palm Canyon

Salton Sea Pupfish (Photograph courtesy of California Department of Fish and Game)

The Visitor Center

WEEKENDER'S GUIDE

Peninsular Bighorn Sheep

View across Borrego Valley from Hellhole Canyon

Montezuma Grade is the portion of County Road S22 that winds down the San Ysidro Mountains.

HELLHOLE CANYON TRAILHEAD

1.1 miles from Visitor Center
0.7 mile south of Palm Canyon Drive
Parking lot is west of and downhill from the road.

The parking lot offers a restroom, information kiosk, and access to three trailheads. The *Little Surprise Canyon Trail* starts at the south edge of the parking lot, just past the restroom. It is an easy 0.75-mile round-trip walk into a short rocky canyon, with fascinating geology and excellent wildflowers in spring. The *Hellhole Canyon Trail* heads west out of the parking lot, starting just beyond the information kiosk. The 2.8-mile trail (one-way) takes you into a wilderness canyon with huge boulders, native palm trees, a hidden waterfall, and a chance to see the endangered bighorn sheep. The *California Riding and Hiking Trail* intersects the Hellhole Trail about a half-mile from the parking lot. A challenging 5.5-mile (one-way) hike will provide some of the most spectacular views of any trail in the park, ultimately arriving at Culp Valley. The information kiosk gives more detailed information about the hikes.

MONTEZUMA VALLEY ROAD

CRAWFORD OVERLOOK

4.5 miles from Visitor Center
0.1 mile past mile marker 12.5, look for call box

At 2,400 feet in elevation, the view from Crawford Overlook encompasses the entire Borrego Valley, Borrego Badlands, Santa Rosa Mountains, Vallecito Mountains, and in clear weather the Salton Sea and Chocolate Mountains 50 miles to the east. Panels mounted atop the stone wall provide general information about the park and bighorn sheep.

After you've enjoyed the eastward view, turn around and look behind you. The rocky slopes in this section of the San Ysidro Mountains are a favorite haunt of the park's most famous animal, bighorn sheep. Study the ridge tops and large protruding rocks (binoculars are helpful, though not required). The sheep like to stand where they have a clear view of the surrounding area. Light tan in color, about the size of a deer, mature bighorns have a distinctive white rump patch and the males have heavy, curling horns. They are often seen here, and on either side of the road for the next three or four miles down the grade.

Desert Agave

The town of Borrego Springs is located at the base of the San Ysidro Mountains in what is called the Borrego Valley. Geologically speaking, the valley is more accurately described as a basin or trough. The San Ysidro and Santa Rosa mountains, on either side of Borrego Springs, are slowly rising, while the valley between them is sinking, creating a basin or structural trough. (A real valley is formed when a river cuts a V-shaped course into the earth.) As this "valley" slowly sinks, sand and gravel eroded from nearby mountains is filling it. Geologists estimate there is presently 5,000 feet of sediment in the trough. The water that has carried sand from the mountains for the last three or four million years has also been stored in the basin. This underground reservoir is the sole source of water for the town of Borrego Springs, and town officials are working hard to protect that supply.

WEEKENDER'S GUIDE

- —— Paved Road
- ═══ Dirt Road
- ---- Foot Trail
- ● Point of Interest
- 🅿 Picnic Area
- ▲ Primitive Camp
- ◀15 Mile Marker

8

These maps only approximate current boundaries.

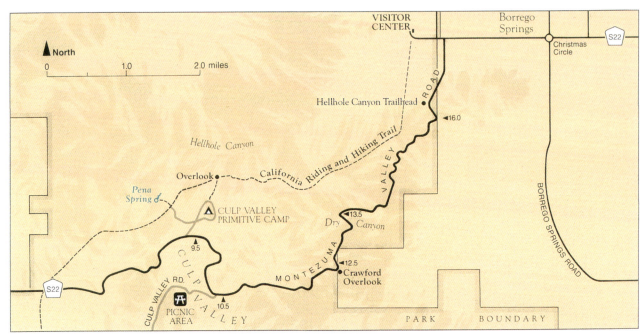

Early morning view of Borrego Valley and the lower ridges of the San Ysidro Mountains from Montezuma Grade

Weather-worn granite boulders in Culp Valley

CULP VALLEY

8.0 miles from Visitor Center
0.25 mile west of mile-marker 9.5
Dirt road: Four-wheel drive not required

The highest campground in the park is located here, as well as a natural spring, an impressive viewpoint, a quiet picnic area, and a portion of the California Riding and Hiking Trail.

At 3,400 feet elevation, Culp Valley Campground can be windy and cold in winter, but a delightfully cool escape from 100-plus degree temperatures of the desert floor in summer. A few hundred yards northeast of the campground a spur of the California Riding and Hiking Trail passes on its descent to the Borrego Valley. A short distance down the trail an overlook offers a rock-framed view of the Borrego Valley, Coyote Mountain, and the Santa Rosa Mountains beyond. A 5.5-mile downhill walk highlighted by scenic views and rich displays of cacti, agave, and perhaps even a bighorn sheep or two, await the hiker who embarks on this portion of the California Riding and Hiking Trail.

Pena Spring is three-quarters of a mile west of the campground. Used heavily by cattle until 1971, this excellent water source now attracts large numbers of birds and other wildlife. Deer and quail are abundant here, and mountain lion and bobcat have been seen nearby. An hour spent quietly near Pena Spring with a pair of binoculars will give impressive proof of the critical value of water in an arid environment. Follow the west fork of the Culp Valley Campground access road 0.3 mile to the parking area. Then continue on foot down the old road until it dead-ends. The spring is a few yards to the west.

To reach Culp Valley Picnic Area, take the Culp Valley Road (dirt) which intersects with the paved road three-fourths mile down the hill from the campground. Follow the dirt road about a half mile west, then make a left turn through big boulders to the picnic area. Small and isolated, this delightful spot is little used. Constructed on the old homesite of an early cattle rancher named Paroli, the picnic area offers shade, cool temperatures, and opportunities for bird-watching and rock scrambling. Like the rest of Culp Valley, this location is studded with piles of huge granite boulders which erode out of the bedrock. The rocks are a favorite lookout of hawks, ravens, and an occasional bobcat.

MONTEZUMA VALLEY ROAD

A thistle blooms in the lush meadow that surrounds Pena Spring.

Bedrock morteros (grinding holes) and prickly pear cactus along the trail to Pena Spring.

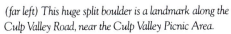

(far left) This huge split boulder is a landmark along the Culp Valley Road, near the Culp Valley Picnic Area.

(left) Reddish-brown seed heads of California buckwheat contrast with cholla cactus near Culp Valley.

WEEKENDER'S GUIDE

Phacelia flowers in Truckhaven Wash

The Truckhaven Rocks are a series of massive sandstone blocks tilted upward when nearby mountains emerged three to four million years ago.

The Truckhaven Trail connected Borrego Springs with communities in the Coachella Valley.

TRUCKHAVEN TRAIL

PEG LEG MONUMENT

9.5 miles from Visitor Center
0.75 mile north of mile-marker 25

There is something magic about gold. Not only can it make you rich if you find enough of it, but it can also make you famous if you lose enough of it. Take Thomas Long "Peg Leg" Smith for example. Born in Kentucky in 1801 with a powerful streak of wanderlust, he joined the Mountain Men at an early age and began a life of adventure. Historians say he was a fur trapper and an Indian fighter; rumor had it that he was a horse thief; most everyone knew him as a storyteller, and a few were of the opinion that he tinkered occasionally with the truth. In 1829 or thereabouts (dates tended to be somewhat flexible with Peg Leg), he brought a load of pelts from Utah to California. On his way through the desert to Los Angeles, he collected some interesting black rocks near the site of present-day Borrego Springs. In Los Angeles they told him the rocks were pure gold.

Well it seems easy to guess what Peg Leg did next. If your guess was a quick trip back to the desert to find the gold, you're right in there with everybody else. But that's not what he did. Instead, he moved to Idaho and got into the horse trading business. Not until 1850, nearly a dozen years after he first found the gold, did he return to California to organize an expedition to relocate his "mine." This search and another in 1853 were unsuccessful. By this time Peg Leg had gotten a bit low on capital and a bit on in years. While his luck at finding gold was poor, he found that talking about gold always drew an audience and a few free drinks. So for the next 13 years, until his death in 1866, Thomas Long "Peg Leg" Smith told stories about his lost gold mine, creating a legend which dominates the folklore of the Old West.

Smoketree

WEEKENDER'S GUIDE

Peg Leg Monument

Smith's stories unleashed a small army of new gold seekers, all looking for his lost mine. Some made up new stories, telling how they had almost found the mine, or found it and then lost it. Some said it was near Borrego, others insisted that it was far to the south, or east, or maybe west. A few even suggested that the only gold Peg Leg ever saw was the kind they poured in his glass.

Enter Harry Oliver, an early resident of Borrego Springs and a retired Hollywood art director. A lover of legends and a good story, Harry started the first Peg Leg Club in 1916. He organized group searches for the mine, and even salted the desert with fake wooden legs to spur more stories. Members of the club met regularly to spin yarns about Peg Leg's adventures and his lost gold. Today a modern version of Harry Oliver's club meets once a year on the first Saturday of April at the Peg Leg Monument on S-22. Known as the Peg Leg Liar's Contest, this annual event falls on the approximate date of Harry's birthday, and is always celebrated with a cake. The public is invited, and anyone may spin a yarn. The rules are simple: the story cannot exceed five minutes, it must have something to do with gold mining in the Southwest, and it must contain nothing which an intelligent person might mistake for the truth. If only Peg Leg could be here now, to see just how far a good story can go.

Just north of Peg Leg Monument, Coyote Mountain juts from the floor of Borrego Valley. Along its face and running northwest into Coyote Canyon is Coyote Creek Fault, the line along which the earth was torn when the mountain emerged. The rocks of Coyote Mountain, and most of those on the monument pile, are metamorphic, that is they were deformed and changed deep within the earth. As the mountain arose, they were brought to the surface. Many contain garnets, small reddish-brown crystals of little or no commercial value, often associated with metamorphic rock. Keep in mind that one of the legends of Peg Leg concerns a most unpleasant ghost who plagues any person who disturbs his rocks.

TRUCKHAVEN TRAIL

11.8 miles from Visitor Center
0.2 mile east of mile-marker 28

In 1929 there was only a single road leading in or out of Borrego Springs. Local residents led by A. A. "Doc" Beaty decided to build a new road connecting Borrego with communities in the Coachella Valley. Construction was accomplished with horses, hand tools, mule-drawn scrapers, and mostly volunteer labor. The difficult project traversed dozens of badlands gullies and canyons, terminating on Highway 99 (later redesignated 86) at a place known as the Truckhaven Cafe. Ironically, just a few days before the heroic project was to be dedicated, flash floods from a summer storm wiped out much of the work.

The paved road which you are driving on today was built in 1968 over the approximate route of the old

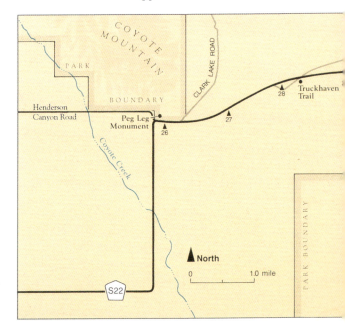

Truckhaven Trail. Known as the Borrego-Salton Seaway, this new road reduces travel time between Borrego Springs and Salton City from three or four hours to about 30 minutes.

While much of the old road is gone, with a bit of searching you may be able to relocate some of the remaining segments. One four-mile section is visible about 2.5 miles east of Peg Leg Monument, where it crosses the pavement and runs northeast just east of mile-marker 28. Loose sand usually makes the old road impassable to any but four-wheel-drive vehicles.

SANTA ROSA OVERLOOK

13.9 miles from Visitor Center
A few yards east of mile-marker 30 a rock wall marks the turnout on the right.

North of this stop the rise from the floor of Clark Valley to the top of Toro Peak (the highest peak visible) is more than 8,000 feet. The Santa Rosa Mountains have emerged quite recently in geologic time (over the last three to four million years) and show all the characteristics of a young mountain range. Their slopes are precipitous, vegetation is minimal or absent, and canyons have rough, jagged outlines. Still rising, the Santa Rosas and their smaller neighbor to the west, Coyote Mountain, are at the center of the San Jacinto Fault Zone, one of California's most active.

The steep slopes and scant vegetation of these youthful mountains provide an ideal setting for greatly accelerated erosion. Rain falling on the exposed flanks of the Santa Rosas flows quickly downhill, picking up loose sand and debris and scouring the fault-fractured surface as it goes. When the water leaves the steep canyons it dumps its load of sand and rocks and boulders on the shallow slopes below. Narrow at the canyon mouth and spreading below, these deposits are called alluvial fans and those at the base of the Santa Rosa

TRUCKHAVEN TRAIL

The Santa Rosa Mountains are characterized by steep, jagged canyons and textbook-perfect alluvial fans.

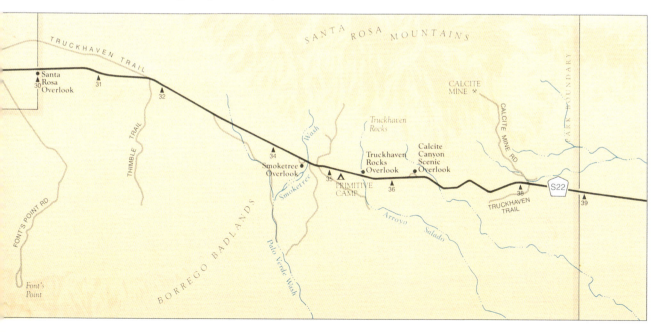

- ——— Paved Road
- ——— Dirt Road
- - - - - - Foot Trail
- • Point of Interest
- ▲ Primitive Camp
- ◂15 Mile Marker

These maps only approximate current boundaries.

WEEKENDER'S GUIDE

A portion of the Borrego Badlands sediments exposed in Palo Verde Wash, near Smoketree Overlook

Tadpole Shrimp

Mountains are textbook-perfect examples of this unique desert landform.

As the Santa Rosa Mountains and Coyote Mountain are shoved up out of the earth, they leave behind an empty space into which Clark Valley, the basin between them, is sinking. If the valley were not sinking, the tremendous volume of alluvial material which it receives from the two mountains would have long since filled it to overflowing, creating a sloping plane or hills instead of the basin you see here. The tremendous weight of the alluvial deposits accelerates the downward movement.

Clark Dry Lake, the lakebed at the bottom of Clark Valley, is an enclosed basin with no outlet, surfaced by clay carried from the surrounding mountains. When floods bring water to the lake, the clay forms a seal preventing it from being absorbed into the ground. With no outlet, and sealed from absorption by the clay, the water stands until evaporation eventually reclaims it. Gambling against the rate of evaporation is a mysterious, prehistoric-looking creature known as the tadpole shrimp. Unseen in the dried clay, the eggs of this unique crustacean hatch when floodwater softens them. Growing quickly to maturity, the inch-long adults then mate and lay more eggs, completing a brief life cycle which is totally dependent on water, one of the desert's most ephemeral components.

Water is the chief sculptor and artist of the landforms you see here. Not only has it carved the canyons and created the alluvial fans, it has also added the rich red patina you see on the mountain's rocks. It has carried the clay which coats the lakebed, and its unique levelling capability has made the lake's surface flatter than any work of man could duplicate. While it is almost never visible, it is responsible for the life cycle of the tadpole shrimp and it maintains the numerous species of plants which live here. The landforms visible from this stop offer an excellent example of the powerful influence water has in a desert environment.

SMOKETREE OVERLOOK

18.3 miles from Visitor Center
Watch closely for the unmarked turnoff, 0.4 miles east of mile-marker 34, turn at call box

Dominated by a field of boulders north of the highway, this view encompasses badlands, mountains, and a sweeping panorama of the park's north end.

To the south are the Vallecito and Fish Creek mountains, and if you look carefully you may be able to pick out the fault which separates them, known as Split Mountain. On the distant south horizon are the Laguna Mountains, rising to over 6,000 feet.

The wrinkled reddish-tan ridges and gullies occupying most of the middle-distance view from south to west comprise the Borrego Badlands. Called badlands by early explorers because of the severe difficulty in traversing them, this austere landscape consists of alternating layers of clay, sand, and gravel deposited by rivers and streams over the last few million years. Rainwater cuts easily into this soft, loosely-packed material forming deep gullies and washes between the ridges.

Watch for white-throated swifts (fast-flying, swallow-like birds), ravens, hawks and occasional golden eagles. Rock wrens and several species of lizards are also seen here. The tall, spiney-armed plants punctuating the landscape are ocotillo, a shrub which is often found on the gentle slopes at the base of desert mountains.

An excellent hike is available nearby. Walk a few yards east along the shoulder of the paved road, then turn left into Smoketree Wash. You'll see dozens of smoke trees and the nearly vertical walls of the wash formed when summer floods cut through soft deposits of mud, sand and cobbles. An excellent place for spring wildflowers, this wash also offers an opportunity to depart the civilized world. A half-hour walk will take you out of sight and sound of any sign of human life, and immerse you in undisturbed desert.

TRUCKHAVEN ROCKS

19.3 miles from Visitor Center
0.5 mile east of mile-marker 35

Like giant turtles breaching from the sea, the Truckhaven Rocks thrust up from the desert floor. Tilted nearly 45 degrees from horizontal, these reddish-brown sandstone blocks are composed of sands and gravels which were washed out of surrounding mountains three to four million years ago.

A little less than a half-mile east of mile-marker 35, you will see the rocks protruding above a sloping field of boulders to the north. Park on the wide shoulder on the north side of the highway adjacent to the drainage channel. Walk west in the drainage channel a few yards until you intersect a sandy wash. Follow the wash upstream about three-quarters of a mile. Abruptly the massive sandstone blocks loom on either side above the steep banks of the arroyo. At this point you may choose to climb out of the wash and scramble up one of the rocks (a strenuous and moderately difficult exercise), or continue up the canyon. Both choices offer great satisfaction.

CALCITE CANYON SCENIC AREA

20.1 miles from Visitor Center
0.2 mile east of mile-marker 36 on left

For several million years prior to the arrival of today's desert climate, streams and rivers in this region carried great loads of gravel and sand from the surrounding mountains. The material was deposited on broad gentle slopes creating alluvial fans. As the fans grew deeper, the tremendous weight of the material on top compressed the layers beneath, consolidating individual particles into coarse sandstone.

Later as the Santa Rosa Mountains began to rise, this entire region was tilted and distorted and the sandstone was fractured in many places. Slow-moving rivers and streams began to flow much faster in response to the steeper slopes and much of the loose material on the surface was carried away. Eventually the sandstone, which had been deeply buried, was uncovered. Water running downhill followed weak places, turning tiny cracks and fissures into grooves and gullies, then channels, and finally huge canyons like the ones below the overlook at this stop.

About ten thousand years ago as the last of the great ice-age glaciers retreated from North America, the desert environment began to evolve in the Southwest. Streams and rivers dried up, and the protective cover of vegetation began to thin. As the climate changed, a pattern of violent summer storms became established. Today seasonal flash floods deliver huge quantities of water in a short time, and with few plants to slow the runoff, erosion proceeds at a frantic pace. A single summer cloudburst can cut 20 feet into the bottom of a gorge or wipe out a thousand smoke trees in two hours.

Two miles east of this stop (turn north a few feet before mile-marker 38) the Calcite Mine Overlook offers yet another view of this upturned landscape. Hidden in a fold of the hills is the site of the Calcite Mine, from which calcite crystals were taken for military use during World War II. A rough dirt road 0.1 mile east of the overlook leads to the mine. Across the highway a section of the old Truckhaven Trail emerges from the badlands. Either of these dirt roads offers an excellent opportunity for a walk into rugged desert. The park's east boundary and the Imperial County line lie three-quarters of a mile to the east, marked clearly by the microwave relay tower. Highway 86 is another 8.5 miles eastward, as are the community of Salton City and the Salton Sea.

TRUCKHAVEN TRAIL

The Truckhaven Rocks, viewed from S22, are named for the Truckhaven Trail.

Seeds spill from the pod of white-stemmed milkweed, a tall slender plant found in the washes of this area.

WEEKENDER'S GUIDE

Western bluebirds are often seen near Yaqui Well.

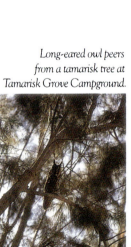

Long-eared owl peers from a tamarisk tree at Tamarisk Grove Campground.

County Road S3 climbs Yaqui Pass on its short route from Highway 78 to Borrego Springs.

YAQUI PASS TRIANGLE

YAQUI PASS AND MESCAL BAJADA OVERLOOKS

12.7 miles from Visitor Center
Yaqui Pass - 0.1 mile south of mile-marker 2 at call box, on left
Mescal Bajada Overlook - 0.1 mile south of mile-marker 1.5, on left

Yaqui Pass is the high point (1,750 feet) along County Road S-3 which runs between Christmas Circle in Borrego Springs and Tamarisk Grove Campground (at Highway 78). Near the pass are a primitive campground, a scenic roadside pullout, and a walking trail. Both the trail and the pullout offer grand views of Mescal Bajada to the south.

The *Kenyon Overlook Trail*, named for an early state park superintendent, begins from Yaqui Pass and is approximately one mile long. After the first quarter mile, a short spur leads to the edge of a steep scarp, offering a spectacular southward view of Mescal Bajada and the nearby Pinyon and Vallecito mountains. For those who prefer not to hike, an alternate but equally impressive overlook may be reached by driving approxi-

Barrel Cactus

mately a half mile south of the pass, to a dirt pullout on the left.

A bajada *(ba ha' da)* is a broad sloping plain at the base of desert mountains. Rainwater falling on these mountains carries mud and debris down steep canyons, then leaves them on more gradual slopes below. The material is deposited in a typical alluvial fan pattern, narrow near the canyon mouth and spreading with distance downslope. When a series of alluvial fans joins in a broad continuous slope, as they have here along the base of the Vallecito Mountains, the resulting landform is called a bajada. Mescal Bajada, named for the desert agave or mescal which inhabit its slopes, is one of the largest in Anza-Borrego.

The *Kenyon Overlook Trail* continues another three-fourths of a mile beyond the overlook to Yaqui Pass Primitive Camp, passing through stands of cacti, agave, creosote bush and jojoba. From the primitive camp it is approximately one-quarter mile back to the trailhead via the road.

WEEKENDER'S GUIDE

— Paved Road
— Dirt Road
-------- Foot Trail
• Point of Interest
▲ Primitive Camp
◀15 Mile Marker

These maps only approximate current boundaries.

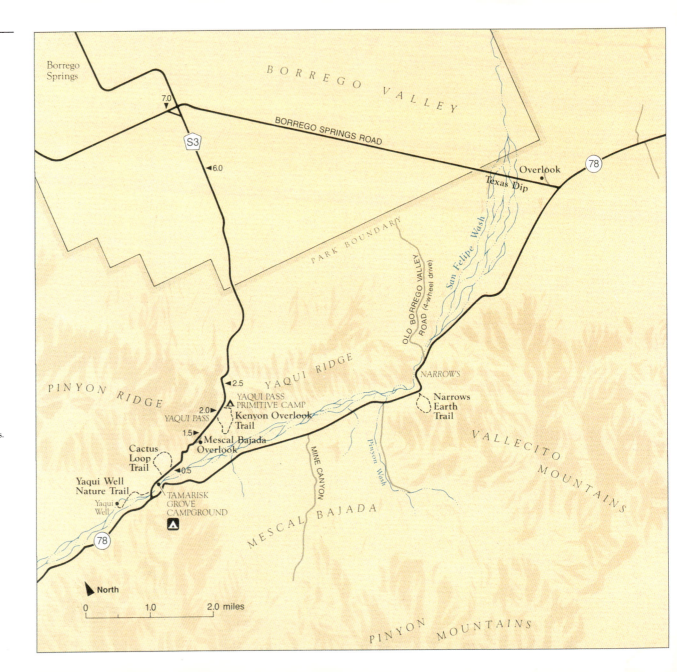

TAMARISK GROVE CAMPGROUND

14.4 miles from Visitor Center
0.1 mile south of mile-marker 0.5

Facilities at Tamarisk Grove, the only campground with shade trees in Anza-Borrego, include drinking water, restrooms and showers, 27 campsites (no hookups), and a small picnic area. At the campground entrance there is a ranger station, visitor information facility, and interpretive display area. A labeled native cactus garden is nearby. Two self-guiding nature trails begin across the road from the entrance: *Cactus Loop Trail* and *Yaqui Well Nature Trail*.

CACTUS LOOP TRAIL

This one-mile loop trail begins a few yards north of the campground entrance. It involves a moderately steep, rocky climb through a rich variety of native cactus species. The northern portion of the trail, just beyond the high point of the loop, offers an outstanding display of hundreds of teddybear cholla. In addition to teddybear and buckhorn cholla, you will see beavertail, barrel, fishhook and hedgehog cacti. In spring wildflower displays often include Bigelow's mimulus, ghost flower, and rock hibiscus. Because of the elevation (nearly 1,500 feet) and prevailing cool winds, the plants here bloom several weeks later than similiar species in lower, warmer locations. If you miss the spring wildflowers in Borrego Palm Canyon, chances are good that plenty can still be seen along this trail.

YAQUI WELL NATURE TRAIL

Less strenuous than the Cactus Loop Trail, Yaqui Well Nature Trail involves approximately two miles of walking. It starts just a few yards south of Tamarisk Grove, and like the Cactus Loop Trail leads through rich populations of cacti, plus ocotillo, mesquite, and other desert shrubs. Signs along the way identify many of the plants.

After you have learned to identify the hedgehog cactus, observe the different colors of spines on different specimens. Individual plants of this fascinating species may have spines varying from gold to black. Like human beings, each plant responds in its own way to genetic and environmental influences, resulting in a few "blondes" here, a few "brunettes" there. Keep your eye on the spines of the barrel cacti as well. They seem to be divided into a "red camp" and a "gold camp." Some botanists have proposed a subspecies or variety of barrel cactus known as "golden barrel," to differentiate it from the more common ones with red or reddish-brown spines.

Fishhook cacti produce cream-colored flowers followed by bright red fruits.

YAQUI PASS TRIANGLE

Beavertail cactus in bloom along the Cactus Loop Trail.

The leaves of ocotillo may turn yellow, orange or even bright red before dropping from the plant during dry seasons.

WEEKENDER'S GUIDE

Teddybear cholla frame this view from the Cactus Loop Trail.

After climbing a couple of easy hills, the trail leads to a natural water hole often used by wildlife. Nearby, Yaqui Well Primitive Camp is popular among campers looking for a quiet retreat, and with bird-watchers. Although the water is too alkaline for human consumption, resident and migratory birds come from far and wide to drink and to perch in the surrounding ironwood trees. The "well" takes its name from a Yaqui Indian who immigrated from Sonora, Mexico, and married a local Diegueño Indian woman.

Beyond Yaqui Well a dirt road follows the pole line and takes the dedicated walker through several more miles of rich cactus stands. This is an excellent route in spring if you seek a place away from the crowds to enjoy the spring wildflowers. From the well, you can return on the trail or follow the dirt road which leads from the primitive camp back to the pavement. The dirt road follows San Felipe Creek, the longest continuous wash in Anza-Borrego. Desert willow, ironwood and mesquite trees grace the broad bed and terraces of this arroyo. You will have several additional opportunities to view San Felipe Creek if you travel east on Highway 78.

Cattails grow in the permanent water of Yaqui Well.

NARROWS EARTH TRAIL

19.5 miles from Visitor Center
4.7 miles east of junction of S-3 and Highway 78

An easy half-mile loop, the Narrows Earth Trail follows the edge of a small alluvial fan while introducing some fascinating aspects of desert geology. Along the way you will encounter rocks nearly 500 million years old, a clearly visible fault line, "salt and pepper" granite, rock flour, and huge ocotillo plants. The trail starts near the east end of the parking area. Self-guiding brochures that explain the geology are available from a dispenser just before stop number 1.

Keep your eyes open for two unusual plants along the trail. Chuparosa, a shrub common on alluvial fans, produces bright red flowers in late winter and early spring. The flowers attract hummingbirds and have led to chuparosa's nickname, "hummingbird plant." Watch for the single specimen here which blooms yellow! Near the end of the trail you will see the darning needle or pencil cholla. This cactus has unusual copper-colored

This fault scarp is clearly visible along the Narrows Earth Trail.

flowers which bloom in late spring, usually in May, and open around two o'clock in the afternoon.

At the high point of the trail loop a narrow, nameless canyon wanders a mile or so back into the hills. If you follow it, you'll find dry waterfalls, massive boulders, dozens of tiny side canyons, sharp turns, steeply sloping side walls, and lots of sand. Though everything is dry, this delightful desert landscape owes its very existence to the single element which is most conspicuously absent — water. Running water has been carving and shaping this little canyon for thousands of years, during brief episodes when summer storms pour torrents of water over the land. In hours the storms are gone, as is the water, leaving only the newly rearranged landscape as evidence of its visit.

Across the highway from the trail, The Narrows, a rocky gorge where San Felipe Creek gets squeezed into a sharp left turn, offers an impressive example of the work of running water. During heavy summer rains this narrow canyon may fill completely with water from dozens of upstream tributaries.

Chuparosa blooms are normally red or orange. Watch for the unusual yellow specimen along the Narrows Earth Trail.

TEXAS DIP

24.0 miles from Visitor Center (via State Highway 78)
8.8 miles east of S-3 on 78, then left on Borrego Springs Rd
0.1 mile west on Borrego Springs Rd to Texas Dip

One mile across and more than 100 feet deep, this section of the San Felipe Creek drainage is a dramatic example of the carving power of water. Try to imagine floodwater extending across the entire floor of this channel. While the mental picture of such a flood may be difficult to imagine, the evidence is inescapable - at some point (or points) in the past, running water carved this mile-wide channel.

There are two explanations of how it might have happened. The old explanation holds that periodic floods, usually occurring during violent summer thunderstorms, have carved the channel over eons of time. A second, more recent theory holds that Texas Dip is a relatively recent feature, and that it may have been carved during a single flooding event. If you came here from the Narrows Earth Trail, you have already passed through the bottleneck canyon known as The Narrows. The new theory proposes that in fairly recent geologic time The Narrows may have acted as a dam, perhaps as a result of earthquake-related landslides that filled the narrow space with rocks and debris. Successive rainstorms formed a lake behind the dam. Then, perhaps resulting from yet another earthquake, the dam was breached and the entire contents of the lake poured through The Narrows as a single, gigantic flood event, carving out the feature we call Texas Dip in a matter of hours.

From its headwaters near the top of San Felipe Valley, along County Road S-2, San Felipe Creek runs for nearly 50 miles before arriving at its final destination, the Salton Sea. Texas Dip stands at about the halfway point on that run.

YAQUI PASS TRIANGLE

San Felipe Creek floods through Texas Dip.

WEEKENDER'S GUIDE

The Vallecito Stage Station was an important stop along the Butterfield Overland Stage route.

Iron door handle, Vallecito Stage Station

The Southern Emigrant Trail

SOUTHERN EMIGRANT TRAIL

SCISSORS CROSSING

21.6 miles from Visitor Center
Junction Highway 78 and County Road S-2

A chapter of California's history was written here, and some of the details are related on two historical monuments which stand near this intersection. San Felipe Creek, the longest watercourse in Anza-Borrego, passes under the bridge here on its 50-mile trip to the Salton Sea.

One mile north of Scissors Crossing on S-2 a trail leads a few yards up onto a rise, where the San Felipe monument is located. You can almost hear the old Butterfield Stage rumbling up San Felipe Valley, its passengers and crew aching to get off at San Felipe Home Station. They have just negotiated one of the most difficult sections along the Southern Emigrant Trail, and the sight of the two-story station with its food, water and shade must have been welcome indeed.

Hoffman's Cholla Cactus

Early the next morning the stage would depart San Felipe Station for the 17-mile, all-day trip to Warner's Ranch. You can drive there today in about 20 minutes. The San Felipe Station is gone now, and a paved highway has replaced the old trail, but you can still find traces of the trail as you drive south on S-2.

County Road S-2 makes a quarter-mile jog to cross San Felipe Creek here, and the result on a map looks like a pair of scissor blades, hence Scissors Crossing. At the point where S-2 turns south from 78 there is a second historical monument, describing the Vallecito Stage Station located 18 miles to the south. (See page 28.)

South of Highway 78 San Felipe Valley takes a new name, one subject to some debate. On maps it is Earthquake Valley, named for the Elsinore Fault which slices through it. Signs at the edge of the small community however, proclaim "Shelter Valley," a name perhaps more attractive to prospective real estate buyers who visit the area.

Scissors Crossing to Campbell Grade Overlook

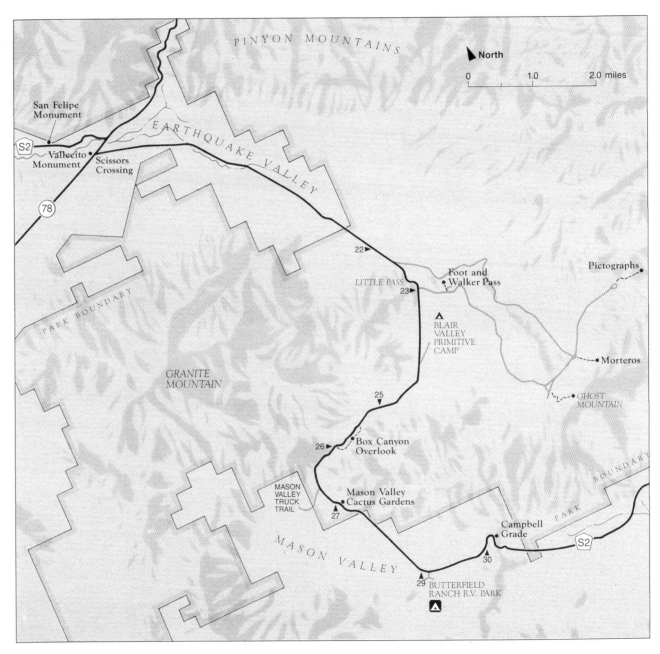

BLAIR VALLEY SIDE TRIP

28.2 miles from Visitor Center
0.9 mile past mile-marker 22
Turn left at Blair Valley sign, left again at information board; take first right and stay right.
Dirt road: Four-wheel drive not required

Historic Foot and Walker Pass, Ghost Mountain (Yaquitepec), Indian Morteros, and the Pictograph Trail are all located along the dirt road which defines Anza-Borrego's largest primitive camping area, Blair Valley. The road is nearly always passable by passenger car, but check conditions first at the Visitor Center. Except for Foot and Walker Pass, each of the places mentioned requires a walk ranging from a half mile to 2.5 miles round-trip.

Foot and Walker Pass (28.9 miles from Visitor Center. Turn left at Historic Marker sign). Stagecoaches from the Butterfield Overland Mail traveled across Blair Valley Dry Lake, and then climbed the rocky ridge at its northern edge. The monument, partway up the ridge, states that the steep gully a few yards to the west was "Foot and Walker Pass" and that the passage was quite difficult. However, more recent research suggests the true route followed the gentler slope to the east. If you look carefully you can find the trace of that old road.

The half mile of dirt road to the base of Foot and Walker Pass is normally passable to any vehicle. It is a 150-foot walk to the top of the pass, and a monument along the way gives a brief history of the pioneers who used this route. From the top of the pass a short trail climbs to a nearby promontory with an outstanding view of Blair Valley and surrounding mountains.

Marshal South Home (Ghost Mountain) is three miles south of Foot and Walker Pass (31.8 miles from Visitor Center). In 1932, Marshal South and his wife Tanya built an adobe home atop the mountain which they called Yaquitepec. All the building materials were obtained locally or hauled in on muleback. They lived there for more than a decade, raising three children and taking care of many of their needs from the surrounding desert. Rainwater was stored in underground cisterns, time was measured on a hand-made sundial, and bread was baked in an outdoor oven. South wrote a series of articles for *Desert Magazine* that described his family's experiment in natural living.

A steep rugged trail leads one mile up the mountain to the remains of the homesite and a panoramic view. Make sure to carry water if you plan to hike this strenuous trail.

The Morteros (32.2 miles from Visitor Center. Follow main road left at Ghost Mountain turnoff to Morteros pullout) are an impressive collection of Indian grinding holes cut into large granitic boulders. An easy quarter-mile trail leads from the parking area to the boulders, which are located at the base of a high ridge. Indian women first hammered out a hollow in the rock surface. Then, over months and years of continued pounding, the hollows grew deeper. Some morteros extend a foot or more into solid rock. Coarse seeds and pods, like the mesquite bean, were pulverized in the grinding holes. After pounding the pods, the women would press the pulp into round cakes and dry them in the sun. Or, if the beans were still green, the moist pulp was put into a clay olla (jar) with water to make a sweet drink.

Chia, white sage, and other fine seeds and delicate plant parts were rubbed or lightly ground into flour on smooth-polished patches of rock known as slicks. A thorough search of rocks in this area, especially those with level surfaces, should reveal several dozen morteros and slicks. The major concentration of grinding surfaces is located near where the trail first approaches the ridge. The rocky canyon that extends eastward beyond the morteros is scenic and seldom visited and well worth an extra half-hour hike.

One-tenth of a mile beyond The Morteros pullout is the road to *Pictograph Trail* (33.8 miles from Visitor

SOUTHERN EMIGRANT TRAIL

Morteros and cholla cactus in Smuggler Canyon near pictograph site

Pictograph, Blair Valley

WEEKENDER'S GUIDE

The Southern Emigrant Trail bypassed this dry waterfall at Box Canyon.

Center). It is rutted and sandy, but is usually passable over its 1.5-mile length. From the parking area the one-mile trail (one way) makes a moderately strenuous climb to the top of a saddle and down the other side to a huge, north-facing boulder marked by a small sign on the right. On the shaded face of the rock are geometric designs painted in faded colors of red and yellow, examples of Indian rock art.

Indian rock art occurs throughout the Southwest and is thought to have been created by shamans or spiritual leaders as part of religious or ceremonial activities. The meanings of the art are obscure, and interpretations vary from one person to another.

A pictograph is painted on a rock surface, while a petroglyph is carved or etched into the rock. Both types are found among the more than 50 known rock art sites in Anza-Borrego. Most of the pictographs in the park are south of Highway 78, while the majority of petroglyphs occur in Anza-Borrego's northern end.

The Pictograph Trail passes through a community of plants seldom seen on the desert floor. Pinyon pine, juniper, nolina, yucca, and white sage are common here, as are a large number of other high-desert shrubs. At 3,200 feet elevation, spring comes late to these mountains. Wildflowers that bloom in the Borrego Valley in March may not open at this elevation until early May. When summer temperatures hit 110 degrees in the valleys, they may barely exceed 90 here.

The trail continues beyond the pictograph site another half mile. Along the trail, several huge, reclining boulders a few yards away from the base of the ridge on the right contain at least two dozen Indian morteros. Farther down the sandy wash, rocky ridges on both sides gradually converge to form a steep-walled canyon. Smuggler Canyon then makes a sharp turn to the right and in a few more feet stops abruptly at a sheer 200-foot drop. Below the dropoff lies a startling view of the Vallecito Valley, the Vallecito Stage Station, and a portion of the old Southern Emigrant Trail, the historic route followed by thousands of immigrants on their way into California.

You can continue northward (to County Road S-2) on the Blair Valley road from the junction at the Pictograph turnoff. However, that route is deeply rutted and unpredictable. The recommended return trip is back the way you came.

BOX CANYON HISTORIC MONUMENT

31.1 miles from Visitor Center
0.75 mile south of mile-marker 25

From the Box Canyon parking area an easy 250-foot trail leads to a view point which looks down on the trail over which thousands of gold-seekers, soldiers, and immigrants walked. Box Canyon, directly below the view point, created a rock barrier requiring the construction of a bypass trail. That trail (the lower of the two across the gorge) is clearly visible and may be reached by following the winding quarter-mile path down from the overlook. Along the way you can look straight down into the "box" of Box Canyon, a vertical rock chute cut by the runoff from thousands of summer storms.

There is something eerie and magical about leaving your own footprints in the same sand which crunched under the boots and wheels of the Mormon Battalion, the 49ers, and the Butterfield Overland Mail. Take a walk down the old trail, back in time to the mid-nineteenth century. What must have filled the minds of immigrants who had never seen a desert, whose main perception of the outdoors was the lush green forests of the East? Imagine what it must have been like to be a traveler here: the fear, the excitement, the dread; wondering what exotic animal or plant would appear around the next bend; whether your wagon would fit between the rocks, and especially when you would next see water.

Geologists estimate that the rock that lines Box Canyon is more than 250 million years old. It is composed of sedimentary layers that were deposited beneath semitropical seas. Over time the weight of thousands of feet of sediments compressed these layers into hard rock. Later the earth buckled as mountains were formed, and the layers were bent and twisted almost beyond recognition. Today they resemble a fine-grained marble cake or multilayered pudding, stirred heavily prior to cooking, then frozen forever.

MASON VALLEY CACTUS GARDENS

32.6 miles from Visitor Center
Park in the large lot on the east side of the road just south of mile-marker 27.

In the north end of Mason Valley are the most extensive populations of native cacti in Anza-Borrego. In places teddybear cholla forms impenetrable thickets; elsewhere five or six different cactus species grow within an arm's length.

Walk about 100 yards east of the parking area, up onto the flat. With a bit of searching you can find prickly pear, hedgehog, fishhook, barrel, and buckhorn and teddybear cholla. Blooming season at this elevation is mid-April to late May.

While most people recognize the danger of cactus spines, few are aware that small pieces of cactus (especially from the teddybear cholla) are often lying loose on the ground. These pieces serve as a reproductive device and will grow a new plant if they are carried to a favorable location by some unsuspecting animal (or human). Examine your shoes periodically as you walk. At the first appearance of a clinging cholla ball, remove it with a pocket comb or two sticks — do not use your hands! Leather shoes or boots are recommended for exploring these superb cactus gardens.

Among the species of cacti to be found in Mason Valley, the teddybear or jumping cholla stands out. It forms the most impressive thickets, usually grows the tallest, has the largest number of spines per square inch, and is the only species with barbed spines. While most cactus spines can be gently pulled out when they penetrate your skin, teddybear's must be ripped out. The "jumping cholla" does not actually jump, but can elicit that response in humans who accidentally touch it!

If you examine a number of teddybear cholla, you will notice that some specimens in Mason Valley have pinkish-tan spines, while the rest bear the more common light yellow spines. Hoffman's teddybear cholla or pink teddybear cholla (Cylindropuntia X Fosbergii) have pink-tan spines and are known to occur only in Anza-Borrego Desert State Park. In addition to the unusual spine color, this species is also taller and more robust than the average teddybear cholla.

The most dramatic photographs of cacti are often made when the sun is low in the sky and comes from behind the plants. To capture this backlight at its best, visit the cacti on the eastern side of the valley in early morning and those on the western slopes late in the afternoon.

CAMPBELL GRADE OVERLOOK

36.1 miles from Visitor Center
0.2 mile south of mile-marker 30

The ridge adjacent to Campbell Grade marks the end of Mason Valley and the beginning of Vallecito Valley. It also was a major barrier along the old Southern Emigrant Trail. Once the ridge at Campbell Grade was climbed, the country became cooler and plants more plentiful. What a relief for travelers who had spent days or weeks riding and walking through barren desert.

Park in the paved pullout on the west side of the road. Very carefully walk across the road and down the shoulder a few yards to the rock promontory. This overlook affords a long view of Vallecito Valley and the distant Carrizo Badlands. A section of the old trail is clearly visible just

SOUTHERN EMIGRANT TRAIL

Cactus gardens, Mason Valley

Hedgehog cactus, Mason Valley

Vallecito Stage Station to Carrizo Badlands Overlook

below, where it climbs up the steep ridge on its way into Mason Valley. On a clear day, Vallecito Stage Station is visible at the far end of Vallecito Valley.

VALLECITO STAGE STATION AND COUNTY PARK

40.8 miles from Visitor Center
Turn off 0.75 mile south of mile-marker 34

A faithfully reconstructed stage station, shady picnic area, campground, historic cemetery, children's playground, and restrooms are all available at this San Diego County park located within Anza-Borrego. A modest day-use fee is charged.

Vallecito was the last stage station at the edge of the desert, offering food, water, shade, and the promise of escape from the desert. Erected in 1857, the station was built from blocks of sod cut from the nearby marsh. These blocks consisted of mud with roots of the marsh plants which, when dried, made a strong, long-lasting building material. Although the original station eventually disintegrated from disuse, it was reconstructed in 1934 using the same material. This authentic, thick-walled replica of the original gives an excellent feel for the accommodations available to travelers in the 1860s.

A forest of mesquite trees surrounds Vallecito. These gnarled desert trees provide indisputable evidence of the abundant water available here. Mesquite, which have long tap roots, are found only where there is permanent water within approximately 60 feet of the surface. Some of the trees are very old, surviving from before the days of the stage station. You can sit under the shade of these trees and imagine the historic characters who came before you: Kumeyaay Indian women gathering mesquite beans, military soldiers assigned to protect the station, travelers from the East Coast on their way to San Fran-

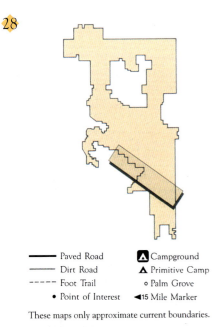

Paved Road — Campground
Dirt Road — Primitive Camp
Foot Trail — Palm Grove
Point of Interest — ◀15 Mile Marker

These maps only approximate current boundaries.

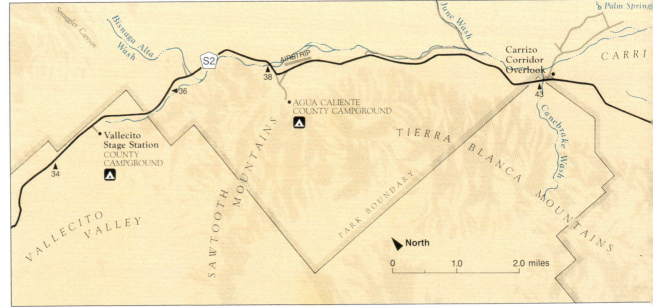

cisco to make a new life, and cowboys tending cattle that grazed in the marsh.

Agua Caliente Hot Springs, a county park, is 3½ miles south of Vallecito, just past mile-marker 38. It offers camping facilities, hot water pools, and restrooms. The pools may be used on a day-use basis for a modest charge. A private concession sells food, snacks and supplies.

CARRIZO CORRIDOR OVERLOOK

49.7 miles from Visitor Center
Park in the pullout on the east side of S-2 at mile-marker 43

The final obstacle of the desert crossing for travelers on the Southern Emigrant Trail was a huge expanse of convoluted ridges and gullies known as the badlands. Travel in a straight line through the badlands was nearly impossible and they were to be avoided at all costs until a permanent path was found through them.

Vallecito Wash, which parallels County Road S-2 for several miles before it turns southeast near this stop, formed the path the pioneers needed. Just a few miles to the southeast Vallecito Wash joins Carrizo and Bow Willow creeks and they all head east toward the Salton Sea. Periodically, summer flash floods transform these dry washes into powerful rivers which have cut the Carrizo Corridor, a path through the badlands which served as a route for thousands of immigrants, soldiers, and wagons entering California in the mid-1800s.

From this unassuming overlook at the turnoff to Palm Spring (across from the tiny community of Canebrake), you can look directly down the Carrizo Corridor. On a hot hazy day, it is easy to imagine the effect such a landscape might have on the minds of eastern travelers accustomed to green trees and abundant streams and rivers. The western edge of the Carrizo Badlands is visible on the far (left) side of the corridor. With sharp eyes or binoculars you may be able to spot a cluster of

SOUTHERN EMIGRANT TRAIL

Interior view, Vallecito Stage Station

A dragonfly rests on a cattail leaf at Palm Spring.

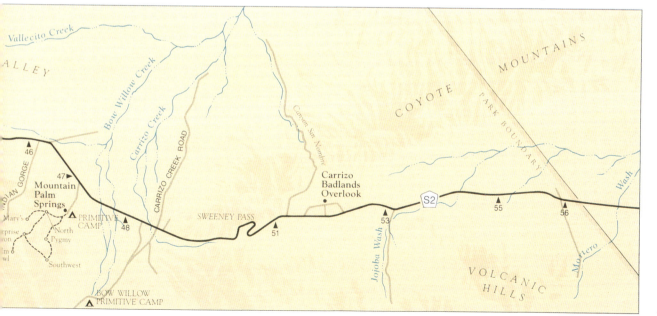

WEEKENDER'S GUIDE

California Fan Palms, North Grove, Mountain Palm Springs

Elephant trees are often seen along the palm grove trail at Mountain Palm Springs.

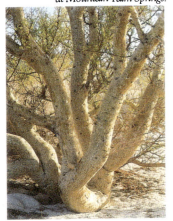

palm trees, due east, at the base of a badlands ridge. These native palms and a historical monument mark the location of Palm Spring, an intermediate stop along the stage line between the Carrizo Station, about 10 miles east, and Vallecito. The spring offered water, though somewhat alkaline, and a bit of shade.

The dirt road heading east to Vallecito Creek is often sandy and not recommended for passenger cars. It is 1.6 miles to the spring, a nice walk on a cool day. Make sure to carry water.

Three and one-half miles south of here on S-2, a prominent sign at a dirt road on the left (east) announces "Great Southern Overland Stage Route of 1849." The sign fails to mention two historical facts: the Butterfield Overland Stage did not use this road (it used the Carrizo Corridor 3½ miles to the north) and the stage operated between 1858 and 1861, not in 1849. So much for history.

MOUNTAIN PALM SPRINGS

54.0 miles from Visitor Center
Just past mile-marker 47
Dirt road: Four-wheel drive not required

At the Mountain Palm Springs turnoff from S-2, look west, using the dirt road as a guide. The Southwest Grove is visible at the base of a rocky ridge about 1½ miles away.

Half a dozen groves of California fan palms and an excellent display of teddybear and Hoffman's cholla are within walking distance of this popular primitive campground. A trail system connects all six groves, and also leads past a number of elephant trees.

As palm trees grow they continually produce new leaves at the top of their trunks. Older leaves wither and eventually die, folding down over the tree's lower section. These "skirts" of dead leaves add a look of fullness and grace to the trees that is typical of the California fan palm, which is named for the shape of its leaves.

Two trails begin at the main parking area, each leading to different palm groves. One trail heads west, up a sandy wash, to the Pygmy and Southwest Groves. Pygmy Grove, named for its short trees, is an easy half-mile walk. Another quarter of a mile brings you to the Southwest Grove, a lush oasis shading a small pool of water. The trail makes a sharp turn north here, heading up a steep ridge to a large elephant tree a few yards above the grove. It then continues north about a half-mile across a rocky hillside toward Surprise Canyon Grove, described below.

The second trail heads north up a sandy and rocky wash, towards four different oases. The first is North Grove, just a half-mile away, and visible from the parking area. Here the trail divides into two forks. The right leads up a rocky ravine about one-third mile to Mary's Grove. The left fork takes you about a half-mile to Surprise Canyon Grove, and then another half-mile to Palm Bowl Grove, flanked by steep, rocky canyon walls. At Surprise Canyon Grove a fork in the trail leads south up a very steep ridge, then across rocky terrain about a half-mile to the Southwest Grove. Refer to the map on page 29.

These small groves offer a fine opportunity to sit in the shade and watch the animals that visit them. Birds especially are abundant around palm trees, and the species seen here include great horned owls, barn owls, white-winged and mourning doves, western and mountain bluebirds, several species of orioles, house finches, and cactus wrens. If you are here in fall, when the tiny fruits of the palms are mature, you can see birds enjoying the sweet, miniature dates. Scientists believe that birds and coyotes help spread the trees by eating the fruit and leaving seed-rich droppings in new locations.

CARRIZO BADLANDS OVERLOOK

58.6 miles from Visitor Center
0.5 mile south of mile-marker 51

As you approach the top of Sweeney Pass, watch closely on the east side of the highway for a sign marking the turnoff to this overlook. A reliable dirt road leads a few yards to the best badlands view in the park's southern end.

The Carrizo Badlands are as impressive as the Borrego Badlands, but because of their remoteness they are not as well known. On a clear day you can look across more than 10 miles of tilted, twisted sedimentary layers dating back nearly five million years. The view also includes a rock formation thought to be the oldest in Anza-Borrego. Below the overlook a dirt road (four-wheel drive only) leads into a canyon. At the point where the road turns left and disappears around a bend, there is an outcrop of dark, coarse rock surrounded by lighter-colored sediments. The dark rock, approximately 500 million years old, forms the backbone of the Coyote Mountains which extend southeast from here. It is composed of sedimentary rock which has been metamorphosed (changed) deep within the earth into finely layered schist, gneiss and marble. Surrounding the ancient metamorphic rock are one- to three-million-year-old sediments which comprise the bulk of the Carrizo Badlands.

As the dirt road turns left, it enters a watercourse with the haunting name of Canyon Sin Nombre, "Canyon Without Name." What has happened to previously horizontal sedimentary layers in this canyon is almost beyond belief. In addition to being tilted upwards at various angles, the layers have in some places actually been bent back over themselves, forming S-shaped curves. In other places the rocks are now vertical. It is possible to travel back a million years in geologic time by walking down Canyon Sin Nombre.

A three-quarter-mile walk will put you into the heart of the canyon. Many short side canyons wind their way between nearly vertical walls and turrets and other unusual formations. All have been carved by that nemesis of badlands sediments, water. Ravens and hawks have built their nests in niches on the walls, and water has created natural bridges and arches. Canyon Sin Nombre offers one of the most satisfying exploring opportunities anywhere in Anza-Borrego. Keep in mind the lack of available water, and the sharp uphill climb on the return to the highway.

Four miles south of the Carrizo Badlands Overlook, County Road S-2 passes through one of Anza-Borrego's few volcanic formations. Watch for a road cut between mile-markers 55 and 56 and some low hills to the west. The rocks on the ground here are andesite and basalt, material which once flowed from volcanoes as molten lava. There are also deposits of volcanic ash that was blown out in a series of eruptions.

It is 4½ miles from the Carrizo Overlook to Anza-Borrego's south boundary, then another eight miles to the community of Ocotillo and the intersection with Interstate 8.

SOUTHERN EMIGRANT TRAIL

Twisted and folded sediments, Canyon Sin Nombre

Leopard Lizard

Badlands ridges and ocotillos, viewed from Carrizo Badlands Overlook

INDEX

Agua Caliente Hot Springs 29
Anza-Borrego Desert State Park 1
Arroyo Salado Primitive Camp 15

Beaty, A.A. "Doc" 12
Bighorn sheep 7
Blair Valley 25, 26
Blair Valley Dry Lake 25
Borrego Badlands 14, 31
Borrego Palm Canyon 2, 3
Borrego Palm Canyon Nature Trail 3
Borrego-Salton Seaway 13
Borrego Springs 7
Borrego Valley 7
Bow Willow Creek 29
Box Canyon 23, 26
Box Canyon Historic Monument 26
Butterfield Overland Mail 25, 26
Butterfield Overland Stage 30
Butterfield Stage 23

Cactus Gardens, Mason Valley 27
Cactus Loop Trail 19
Calcite Canyon Scenic Area 15
Calcite Mine Overlook 15
California Riding and Hiking Trail 9
Campbell Grade Overlook 27
Campfire Center 5
Canebrake 29
Canyon Sin Nombre 31
Carrizo Badlands 27, 29, 31
Carrizo Badlands Overlook 31
Carrizo Corridor 29, 30
Carrizo Corridor Overlook 29
Carrizo Creek 29
Carrizo Station 30
Christmas Circle 17
Clark Dry Lake 14
Clark Valley 13, 14
Coyote Creek Fault 12

Coyote Mountain 12, 13, 14
Coyote Mountains 31
Crawford Overlook 7
Culp Valley 9
Culp Valley Campground 9
Culp Valley Picnic Area 9

Earthquake Valley 23

Fish Creek Mountains 14
Foot and Walker Pass 23, 25
49ers 26

Garden, Newt and Mary Ann Williams 3
Ghost Mountain 25
Great Southern Overland Stage Route 30
Grove, Mary's 30
Grove, North 30
Grove, Palm Bowl 30
Grove, Pygmy 30
Grove, Southwest 30
Grove, Surprise Canyon 30

Hot Springs, Agua Caliente 29

Kenyon Overlook Trail 17

Laguna Mountains 14

Mary's Grove 30
Mason Valley 27, 28
Mason Valley Cactus Gardens 27
Mescal Bajada 17
Mescal Bajada Overlook 17
Montezuma Valley Road 7
Mormon Battalion 26
Morteros, The 25
Mountain Palm Springs 30

Narrows, The 21
Narrows Earth Trail 20
Newt and Mary Ann Williams Garden 3
North Grove 30

Ocotillo 31
Oliver, Harry 12

Palm Bowl Grove 30
Palm Spring 29, 30
Panoramic Overlook Trail 3
Park Headquarters 5
Peg Leg Liar's Contest 12
Peg Leg Monument 11
Peg Leg Smith 11
Pena Spring 9
Picnic Area, Borrego Palm Canyon 5
Picnic Area, Culp Valley 9
Pictograph Trail 25, 26
Pinyon Mountains 17
Pupfish 5
Pupfish Sanctuaries 5
Pygmy Grove 30

Salton City 13, 15
Salton Sea 15, 21, 29
San Felipe Creek 20, 21, 23
San Felipe Home Station 23
San Felipe Valley 23
San Felipe Valley Fault 23
San Jacinto Fault Zone 13
Santa Rosa Mountains 7, 13, 14
Santa Rosa Overlook 13
San Ysidro Mountains 7
Scissors Crossing 23
Shelter Valley 23
Shrimp, tadpole 14
Smith, Peg Leg 11
Smoketree Overlook 14

Smoketree Wash 14
Smuggler Canyon 26
Southern Emigrant Trail 23, 26, 27, 29
South, Marshal 25
South, Tanya 25
Southwest Grove 30
Split Mountain 14
Surprise Canyon Grove 30
Sweeney Pass 31

Tamarisk Grove Campground 17, 19
Texas Dip 21
Toro Peak 13
Truckhaven Rocks 15
Truckhaven Trail 11, 12, 15

Vallecito County Park 28
Vallecito Creek 30
Vallecito Mountains 14, 17
Vallecito Stage Station 23, 26, 28, 30
Vallecito Valley 26, 27, 28
Vallecito Wash 29
Visitor Center-Campground Trail 5
Visitor Center Loop Trail 5

Walking Trails 3, 5, 9, 17, 19, 20, 25, 26, 30
Warner's Ranch 23

Yaqui Pass Overlook 17
Yaqui Pass Primitive Camp 17
Yaquitepec 25
Yaqui Well Nature Trail 19
Yaqui Well Primitive Camp 20